W9-DDK-084

SCHOLASTIC

Sight Word Trees

New York · Toronto · London · Auckland · Sydney
Mexico City · New Delhi · Hong Kong · Buenos Aires

Teaching *Resources*

Edited by Immacula A. Rhodes

Cover design by Scott Davis

Interior design by Sydney Wright

Illustrations by Teresa Anderko, Maxie Chambliss,
Kate Flanagan, Rusty Fletcher, and Sydney Wright

ISBN: 978-0-545-53833-6
Text and illustrations © 2013 by Scholastic Inc.
All rights reserved. Published by Scholastic Inc.
Printed in the U.S.A..

6 7 8 9 10   40   20 19 18 17

Contents

Sight Word Trees

Sight Words

Introduction

Sight Word Trees offers an engaging and fun way for kids to master more than 50 high-frequency words found on the Dolch Basic Sight Word Vocabulary List, which accounts for more than 50% of the words found in textbooks today. In his book *Phonics From A to Z* (Scholastic, 2006, revised), reading specialist Wiley Blevins notes that the benefits of having a bank of sight words at the ready are significant for children who are learning to read. Accurate and automatic recognition of sight words enables a child to read more smoothly and at a faster rate, helping the child remember more of what he or she has just read and make sense of it. This is vital in order for young children to become fluent readers and comprehend the text they read.

The activities in this book give children lots of practice in reading sight words in context. In addition to repeated exposure to target words, picture clues help children attach meaning to the sentences they read. And writing the missing words to complete the sentences helps reinforce sight-word spellings and provides the opportunity for children to develop phonemic awareness skills.

You can use the sight word trees with the whole class or in small groups. Or place them in a learning center for children to use independently or in pairs. The activities are ideal for children of all learning styles, ELL students, and for RTI instruction. And best of all, the sight word trees take only a few minutes to complete, making them a quick way to integrate recognition of high-frequency words into the school day.

How to Use the Sight Word Trees

Completing a sight word tree is easy and fun. To begin, distribute copies of the activity page for the word you want to teach. Point out the word on the basket that's under the tree and name it. Then have children do the following:

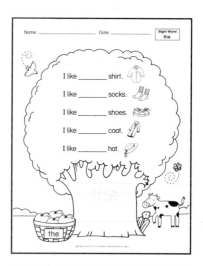

1 Trace the sight word on the top line on the tree trunk. Then write the word on the bottom line.

2 Complete each sentence on the tree by writing the sight word on the blank line.

3 Read each sentence aloud, pointing to each word while saying it.

Check pages 6–8 for a list of sentences that can be created with each sight word.

Activities to Extend Learning

Use these activities to give children additional opportunities to practice sight word recognition.

Make Your Own Tree: Use the template on page 64 to create your own sight word trees. To prepare, choose a word to feature on the page. Print a model of that word on the top line on the trunk. Write short sentences that include the feature word on the tree, using a blank line in place of the word. If desired, refer to pages 6–8 to find a series of sentences that might work with your target sight word. For instance, the sentences on page 12 (for the sight word *he*) can also be used to give children practice with *how*. As a comprehension aid, you might draw or glue a picture next to each sentence. Then copy a class supply of the page, distribute to children, and have them complete the activity. You might also give copies of the template to children so they can make their own sight word trees.

Sight Word Apples: Label a supply of red apple cutouts with different sight words. Put the apples in a learning center. Then have student pairs use the apples as flash cards. One child can hold up one card at a time as the other child reads the word on it. To extend, have children work together to put the words in alphabetical order.

Sight Word Shape Books: For shape books, make colored copies of the tree template (page 64) on sturdy paper. Also, cut a class supply of plain paper into quarters. To make a book, have children cut out the tree, then stack and staple 6–8 pages to the treetop. Ask them to choose a sight word (or assign words to children) and write it on the lines on the tree trunk. Then have children write a different sentence on each page, using their word in each sentence. If desired, they can also illustrate their sentences. Invite children to read their completed shape books with partners.

Sight Word Memory: To make game cards for this familiar game, choose 10–12 sight words. Create apple-shaped cutouts on red paper and label one pair of cutouts with each of the words (you'll have 20–24 apples in all). Then invite children to use the cards to play Memory. Each time they find the two apples labeled with the same sight word, they keep the match.

Musical Word Walk: Label sheets of paper with sight words, preparing two sheets for each sight word you plan to use in the activity. Arrange the sheets word-side down in a looped path. Then have children walk along the outside of the path while music plays. Periodically stop the music, have children pick up the nearest sheet, and then find another child with the sheet that has the matching word.

Connections to the Common Core State Standards

The Common Core State Standards Initiative (CCSSI) has outlined learning expectations in English Language Arts for students at different grade levels. The activities in this book align with the following Foundational Skills for Reading for students in grades K–2. For more information, visit the CCSSI Web site at www.corestandards.org.

Print Concepts

RF.K.1, RF.1.1. Demonstrate understanding of the organization and basic features of print.
RF.K.1a, RF.K.1b, RF.K.1c
RF.1.1a

Phonological Awareness

RF.K.2, RF.1.2. Demonstrate understanding of spoken words, syllables, and sounds (phonemes).

Phonics and Word Recognition

RF.K.3, RF.1.3, RF.2.3. Know and apply grade-level phonics and word analysis skills in decoding words.
RF.K.3c
RF.1.3g
RF.2.3f

Fluency

RF.K.4. Read emergent-reader texts with purpose and understanding.
RF.1.4, RF.2.4. Read with sufficient accuracy and fluency to support comprehension.
RF.1.4a, RF.1.4b, RF.1.4c
RF.2.4a, RF.2.4b, RF.2.4c

the *(page 9)*
I like **the** shirt.
I like **the** socks.
I like **the** shoes.
I like **the** coat.
I like **the** hat.

to *(page 10)*
Let's go **to** the zoo.
Let's go **to** the library.
Let's go **to** the park.
Let's go **to** the store.
Let's go **to** the beach.

and *(page 11)*
We eat ham **and** eggs.
We eat meat **and** potatoes.
We eat cheese **and** crackers.
We eat apples **and** bananas.
We eat rice **and** beans.

he *(page 12)*
See how **he** runs.
See how **he** throws.
See how **he** catches.
See how **he** jumps.
See how **he** swims.

a *(page 13)*
Here is **a** book.
Here is **a** pencil.
Here is **a** crayon.
Here is **a** block.
Here is **a** puzzle.

I *(page 14)*
I have a cat.
I have a dog.
I have a bird.
I have a fish.
I have a turtle.

you *(page 15)*
This pie is for **you**.
This cake is for **you**.
This cupcake is for **you**.
This doughnut is for **you**.
This cookie is for **you**.

it *(page 16)*
You see with **it**.
You hear with **it**.
You smell with **it**.
You taste with **it**.
You feel with **it**.

of *(page 17)*
I have lots **of** cards.
I have lots **of** jacks.
I have lots **of** marbles.
I have lots **of** blocks.
I have lots **of** pennies.

in *(page 18)*
The mouse is **in** the hat.
The mouse is **in** the box.
The mouse is **in** the basket.
The mouse is **in** the cup.
The mouse is **in** the shoe.

was *(page 19)*
He **was** sad.
He **was** happy.
He **was** scared.
He **was** tired.
He **was** mad.

said *(page 20)*
"Hello," **said** the nurse.
"Hello," **said** the teacher.
"Hello," **said** the dentist.
"Hello," **said** the firefighter.
"Hello," **said** the artist.

his *(page 21)*
This is **his** bat.
This is **his** ball.
This is **his** glove.
This is **his** cap.
This is **his** shirt.

that *(page 22)*
I want **that** car.
I want **that** bear.
I want **that** duck.
I want **that** puzzle.
I want **that** top.

she *(page 23)*
Does **she** like bugs?
Does **she** like flowers?
Does **she** like butterflies?
Does **she** like leaves?
Does **she** like snakes?

for *(page 24)*
The gift is **for** you.
The hat is **for** you.
The horn is **for** you.
The cake is **for** you.
The sign is **for** you.

on *(page 25)*
A hen is **on** the box.
A turtle is **on** the box.
A dog is **on** the box.
A cat is **on** the box.
A frog is **on** the box.

they *(page 26)*
See how **they** sing.
See how **they** march.
See how **they** dance.
See how **they** jump.
See how **they** play.

but *(page 27)*
I have paper, **but** no paint.
I have paper, **but** no pencil.
I have paper, **but** no crayons.
I have paper, **but** no markers.
I have paper, **but** no pens.

had *(page 28)*
They **had** fries.
They **had** chips.
They **had** popcorn.
They **had** crackers.
They **had** pretzels.

at *(page 29)*
We are **at** the library.
We are **at** the school.
We are **at** the post office.
We are **at** the police station.
We are **at** the fire station.

Sight Word Trees © 2013 by Scholastic Teaching Resources

(continued)

him *(page 30)*
Watch **him** ride.
Watch **him** skate.
Watch **him** throw.
Watch **him** slide.
Watch **him** climb.

with *(page 31)*
Knit **with** your hands.
Clap **with** your hands.
Build **with** your hands.
Write **with** your hands.
Wave **with** your hands.

up *(page 32)*
A bird goes **up**.
A plane goes **up**.
A balloon goes **up**.
A helicopter goes **up**.
A rocket goes **up**.

all *(page 33)*
I drank **all** the milk.
I drank **all** the juice.
I drank **all** the water.
I drank **all** the tea.
I drank **all** the soda.

look *(page 34)*
Come **look** at the TV.
Come **look** at the picture.
Come **look** at the computer.
Come **look** at the puzzle.
Come **look** at the book.

is *(page 35)*
This **is** my table.
This **is** my chair.
This **is** my desk.
This **is** my bed.
This **is** my stool.

her *(page 36)*
She played with **her** car.
She played with **her** bear.
She played with **her** jacks.
She played with **her** doll.
She played with **her** top.

there *(page 37)*
A quilt is in **there**.
A frame is in **there**.
A lamp is in **there**.
A tray is in **there**.
A fan is in **there**.

some *(page 38)*
Have **some** pizza.
Have **some** oatmeal.
Have **some** spaghetti.
Have **some** yogurt.
Have **some** salad.

out *(page 39)*
Hang **out** the socks.
Hang **out** the shirt.
Hang **out** the pants.
Hang **out** the dress.
Hang **out** the shorts.

as *(page 40)*
I'm as fast **as** a deer.
I'm as fast **as** a horse.
I'm as fast **as** a squirrel.
I'm as fast **as** a giraffe.
I'm as fast **as** a dog.

be *(page 41)*
I want to **be** a clown.
I want to **be** a lion tamer.
I want to **be** a bandleader.
I want to **be** a ringmaster.
I want to **be** an acrobat.

have *(page 42)*
Birds **have** feet.
Birds **have** eyes.
Birds **have** wings.
Birds **have** tails.
Birds **have** beaks.

go *(page 43)*
Let's **go** on a bus.
Let's **go** on a train.
Let's **go** on a boat.
Let's **go** on a plane.
Let's **go** on a bike.

we *(page 44)*
Can **we** visit a city?
Can **we** visit a farm?
Can **we** visit a museum?
Can **we** visit a circus?
Can **we** visit a zoo?

am *(page 45)*
I **am** hot.
I **am** tall.
I **am** cold.
I **am** short.
I **am** big.

then *(page 46)*
I read **then** eat.
I read **then** sleep.
I read **then** play.
I read **then** clean.
I read **then** write.

little *(page 47)*
See the **little** pig.
See the **little** duck.
See the **little** sheep.
See the **little** bear.
See the **little** cow.

down *(page 48)*
Go **down** the hill.
Go **down** the slide.
Go **down** the stairs.
Go **down** the ladder.
Go **down** the road.

do *(page 49)*
Let's **do** a flip.
Let's **do** a dance.
Let's **do** a march.
Let's **do** a song.
Let's **do** a play.

can *(page 50)*
I **can** bark.
I **can** oink.
I **can** moo.
I **can** squeak.
I **can** tweet.

Sight Word Sentence Lists

(continued)

could *(page 51)*
We **could** ski.
We **could** surf.
We **could** skate.
We **could** sled.
We **could** ride.

when *(page 52)*
I rest **when** I'm tired.
I eat **when** I'm hungry.
I drink **when** I'm thirsty.
I smile **when** I'm happy.
I wash **when** I'm dirty.

did *(page 53)*
He **did** wash the dishes.
He **did** sweep the floors.
He **did** wipe the windows.
He **did** clean the rugs.
He **did** dust the furniture.

what *(page 54)*
I know **what** flies.
I know **what** swims.
I know **what** crawls.
I know **what** slithers.
I know **what** runs.

so *(page 55)*
Her hair is **so** curly.
His hair is **so** short.
His hair is **so** straight.
Her hair is **so** dark.
Her hair is **so** long.

see *(page 56)*
We **see** a lion.
We **see** a monkey.
We **see** an elephant.
We **see** a zebra.
We **see** a giraffe.

not *(page 57)*
Do **not** go.
Do **not** walk.
Do **not** enter.
Do **not** ride.
Do **not** park.

were *(page 58)*
Where **were** the boots?
Where **were** the flip-flops?
Where **were** the slippers?
Where **were** the sandals?
Where **were** the shoes?

get *(page 59)*
We want to **get** pizza.
We want to **get** chicken.
We want to **get** ice cream.
We want to **get** burgers.
We want to **get** hot dogs.

them *(page 60)*
Look at **them** race.
Look at **them** play.
Look at **them** hide.
Look at **them** dance.
Look at **them** build.

like *(page 61)*
I **like** to read.
I **like** to play.
I **like** to draw.
I **like** to sing.
I **like** to laugh.

one *(page 62)*
I see **one** sun.
I see **one** moon.
I see **one** star.
I see **one** planet.
I see **one** cloud.

this *(page 63)*
Use **this** cup.
Use **this** plate.
Use **this** spoon.
Use **this** fork.
Use **this** bowl.

Name: _____ Date: _____

I like _____ shirt.

I like _____ socks.

I like _____ shoes.

I like _____ coat.

I like _____ hat.

the

Sight Word Trees © 2013 by Scholastic Teaching Resources, page 9

Name: _____ Date: _____

Let's go _____ the zoo.

Let's go _____ the library.

Let's go _____ the park.

Let's go _____ the store.

Let's go _____ the beach.

to

Name: _____ Date: _____

We eat ham _____ eggs.

We eat meat _____ potatoes.

We eat cheese _____ crackers.

We eat apples _____ bananas.

We eat rice _____ beans.

and

Name: _____ Date: _____

See how _____ runs.

See how _____ throws.

See how _____ catches.

See how _____ jumps.

See how _____ swims.

he

he

Name: _____ Date: _____

Here is _____ book.

Here is _____ pencil.

Here is _____ crayon.

Here is _____ block.

Here is _____ puzzle.

_____ have a cat.

_____ have a dog.

_____ have a bird.

_____ have a fish.

_____ have a turtle.

I

This pie is for _____ .

This cake is for _____ .

This cupcake is for _____ .

This doughnut is for _____ .

This cookie is for _____ .

you

you

Name: _____ Date: _____

You see with _____.

You hear with _____.

You smell with _____.

You taste with _____.

You feel with _____.

it

Name: _____ Date: _____

I have lots _____ cards.

I have lots _____ jacks.

I have lots _____ marbles.

I have lots _____ blocks.

I have lots _____ pennies.

of

Name: _____ Date: _____

The mouse is _____ the hat.

The mouse is _____ the box.

The mouse is _____ the basket.

The mouse is _____ the cup.

The mouse is _____ the shoe.

in

in

Name: _____ Date: _____

He _____ sad.

He _____ happy.

He _____ scared.

He _____ tired.

He _____ mad.

was

was

Name: _____ Date: _____

"Hello," _____ the nurse.

"Hello," _____ the teacher.

"Hello," _____ the dentist.

"Hello," _____ the firefighter.

"Hello," _____ the artist.

said

said

Name: _____ Date: _____

This is _____ bat.

This is _____ ball.

This is _____ glove.

This is _____ cap.

This is _____ shirt.

his

his

Name: _____ Date: _____

I want _____ car.

I want _____ bear.

I want _____ duck.

I want _____ puzzle.

I want _____ top.

that

Does _____ like bugs?

Does _____ like flowers?

Does _____ like butterflies?

Does _____ like leaves?

Does _____ like snakes?

she

she

Name: _____   Date: _____

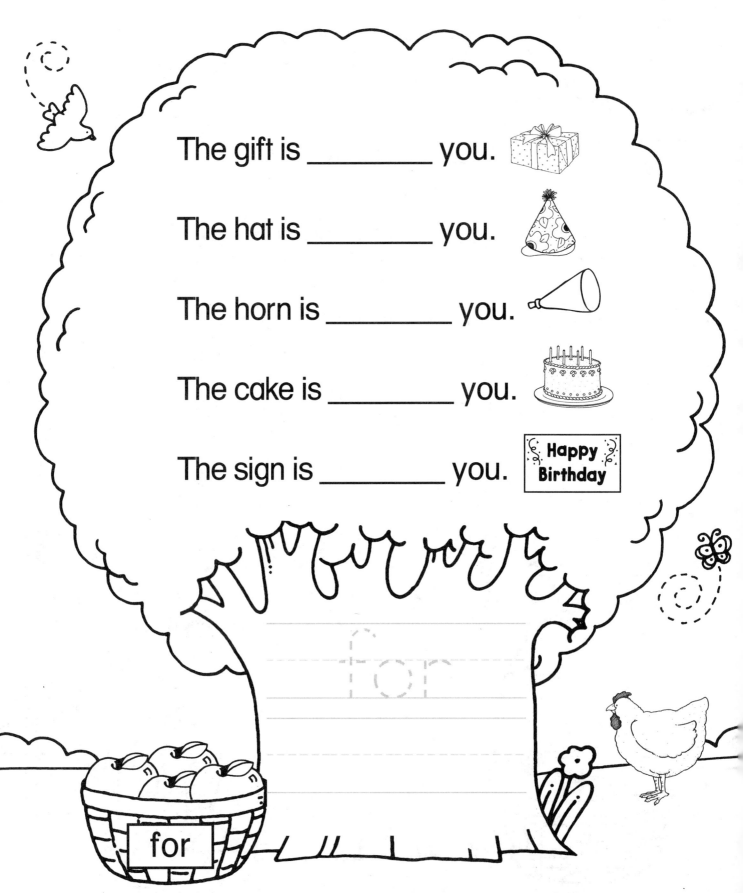

The gift is _____ you.

The hat is _____ you.

The horn is _____ you.

The cake is _____ you.

The sign is _____ you.

Happy Birthday

for

for

Name: _____ Date: _____

A hen is _____ the box.

A turtle is _____ the box.

A dog is _____ the box.

A cat is _____ the box.

A frog is _____ the box.

on

on

Name: _____   Date: _____

See how _____ sing.

See how _____ march.

See how _____ dance.

See how _____ jump.

See how _____ play.

they

they

I have paper, _____ no paint.

I have paper, _____ no pencil.

I have paper, _____ no crayons.

I have paper, _____ no markers.

I have paper, _____ no pens.

but

but

Name: _____ Date: _____

They _____ fries.

They _____ chips.

They _____ popcorn.

They _____ crackers.

They _____ pretzels.

had

Name: _____ Date: _____

We are _____ the library.

We are _____ the school.

We are _____ the post office.

We are _____ the police station.

We are _____ the fire station.

at

at

Name: _____ Date: _____

Watch _____ ride.

Watch _____ skate.

Watch _____ throw.

Watch _____ slide.

Watch _____ climb.

him

Name: _____ Date: _____

Knit _____ your hands.

Clap _____ your hands.

Build _____ your hands.

Write _____ your hands.

Wave _____ your hands.

with

with

Name: _____ Date: _____

A bird goes _____.

A plane goes _____.

A balloon goes _____.

A helicopter goes _____.

A rocket goes _____.

up

Name: _____ Date: _____

I drank _____ the milk.

I drank _____ the juice.

I drank _____ the water.

I drank _____ the tea.

I drank _____ the soda.

all

Come _____ at the TV.

Come _____ at the picture.

Come _____ at the computer.

Come _____ at the puzzle.

Come _____ at the book.

PUZZLE

The Three Bears

look

Name: _____ Date: _____

This _____ my table.

This _____ my chair.

This _____ my desk.

This _____ my bed.

This _____ my stool.

is

is

Name: _____ Date: _____

She played with _____ car.

She played with _____ bear.

She played with _____ jacks.

She played with _____ doll.

She played with _____ top.

her

Name: _____ Date: _____

A quilt is in _____.

A frame is in _____.

A lamp is in _____.

A tray is in _____.

A fan is in _____.

there

Name: _____ Date: _____

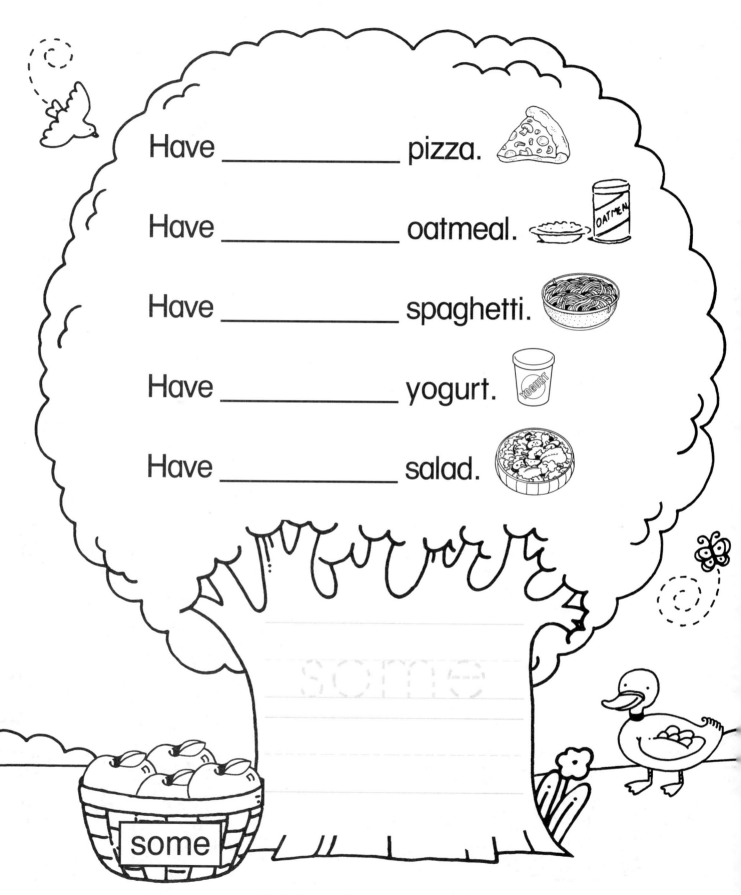

Have _____ pizza.

Have _____ oatmeal.

Have _____ spaghetti.

Have _____ yogurt.

Have _____ salad.

some

some

Name: _____ Date: _____

Hang _____ the socks.

Hang _____ the shirt.

Hang _____ the pants.

Hang _____ the dress.

Hang _____ the shorts.

out

out

I'm as fast _____ a deer.

I'm as fast _____ a horse.

I'm as fast _____ a squirrel.

I'm as fast _____ a giraffe.

I'm as fast _____ a dog.

as

Name: _____ Date: _____

I want to _____ a clown.

I want to _____ a lion tamer.

I want to _____ a bandleader.

I want to _____ a ringmaster.

I want to _____ an acrobat.

be

be

Name: _____ Date: _____

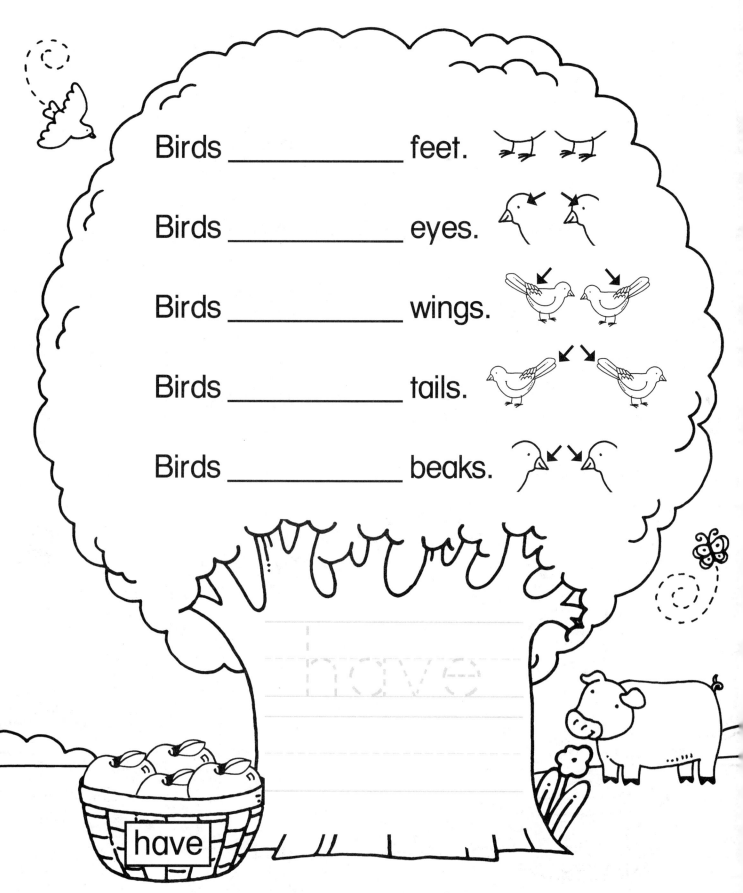

Birds _____ feet.

Birds _____ eyes.

Birds _____ wings.

Birds _____ tails.

Birds _____ beaks.

have

Name: _____ Date: _____

Let's _____ on a bus.

Let's _____ on a train.

Let's _____ on a boat.

Let's _____ on a plane.

Let's _____ on a bike.

go

go

Name: _____ Date: _____

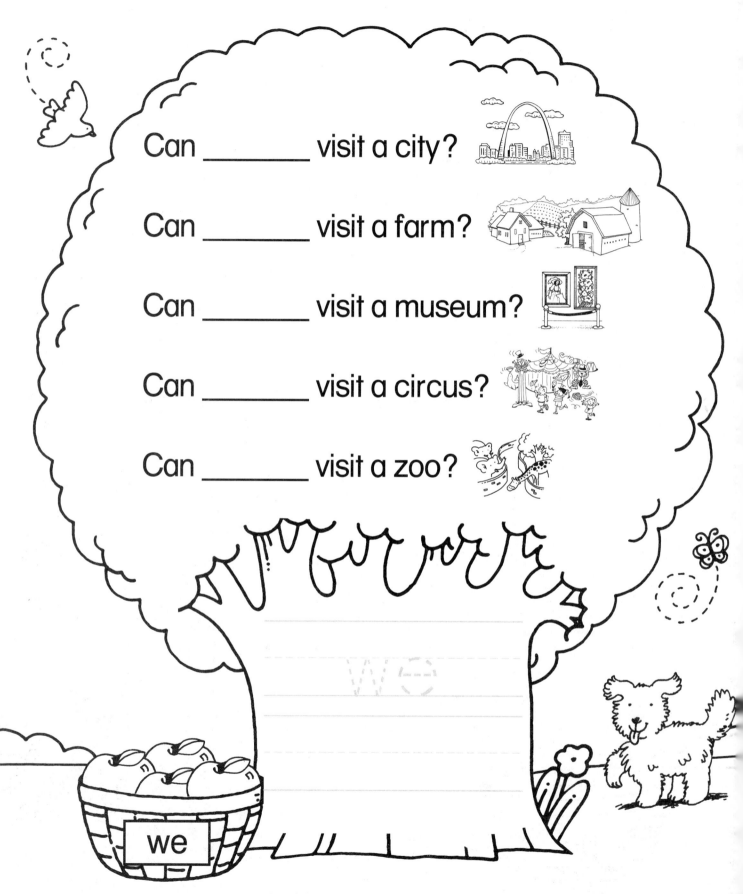

Can _____ visit a city?

Can _____ visit a farm?

Can _____ visit a museum?

Can _____ visit a circus?

Can _____ visit a zoo?

we

Name: _____ Date: _____

I _____ hot.

I _____ tall.

I _____ cold.

I _____ short.

I _____ big.

am

am

Name: _____ Date: _____

I read _____ eat.

I read _____ sleep.

I read _____ play.

I read _____ clean.

I read _____ write.

then

then

Name: _____ Date: _____

See the _____ pig.

See the _____ duck.

See the _____ sheep.

See the _____ bear.

See the _____ cow.

little

Go _____ the hill.

Go _____ the slide.

Go _____ the stairs.

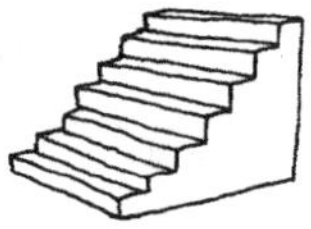

Go _____ the ladder.

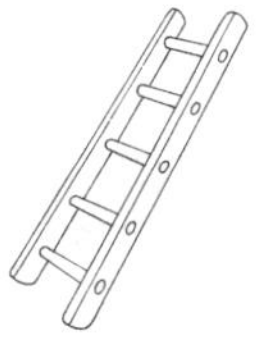

Go _____ the road.

down

down

Name: _____ Date: _____

Let's _____ a flip.

Let's _____ a dance.

Let's _____ a march.

Let's _____ a song.

Let's _____ a play.

do

Name: _____ Date: _____

I _____ bark.

I _____ oink.

I _____ moo.

I _____ squeak.

I _____ tweet.

can

Name: _____ Date: _____

We _____ ski.

We _____ surf.

We _____ skate.

We _____ sled.

We _____ ride.

could

could

Name: _____ Date: _____

I rest _____ I'm tired.

I eat _____ I'm hungry.

I drink _____ I'm thirsty.

I smile _____ I'm happy.

I wash _____ I'm dirty.

when

when

He _____ wash the dishes.

He _____ sweep the floors.

He _____ wipe the windows.

He _____ clean the rugs.

He _____ dust the furniture.

did

did

Name: _____ Date: _____

I know _____ flies.

I know _____ swims.

I know _____ crawls.

I know _____ slithers.

I know _____ runs.

what

what

Her hair is _____ curly.

His hair is _____ short.

His hair is _____ straight.

Her hair is _____ dark.

Her hair is _____ long.

SO

SO

We _____ a lion.

We _____ a monkey.

We _____ an elephant.

We _____ a zebra.

We _____ a giraffe.

see

see

Do _____ go.

Do _____ walk.

Do _____ enter.

Do _____ ride.

Do _____ park.

not

not

Name: _____ Date: _____

Where _____ the boots?

Where _____ the flip-flops?

Where _____ the slippers?

Where _____ the sandals?

Where _____ the shoes?

were

were

Name: _____ Date: _____

We want to _____ pizza.

We want to _____ chicken.

We want to _____ ice cream.

We want to _____ burgers.

We want to _____ hot dogs.

get

Name: _____ Date: _____

Look at _____ race.

Look at _____ play.

Look at _____ hide.

Look at _____ dance.

Look at _____ build.

them

them

Name: _____ Date: _____

I _____ to read.

I _____ to play.

I _____ to draw.

I _____ to sing.

I _____ to laugh.

like

Name: _____ Date: _____

I see _____ sun.

I see _____ moon.

I see _____ star.

I see _____ planet.

I see _____ cloud.

one

Use _____ cup.

Use _____ plate.

Use _____ spoon.

Use _____ fork.

Use _____ bowl.

this

this

Name: _____ Date: _____